About this Book

Color - Cut - Create

1. *Color* in the 50 States of America

Grab your coloring pencils or crayons and get to work making your unique map. Each State is represented by an animal, flower or object. Patterns range from beginner to advanced.

2. *Cut* out your Unique States

Grab a sissors & get to work cutting out the 50 states. Border lines are smooth to ensure cutting is made easy.

3. *Create* My United States Map

Join each of the states together to create a colorful & beautiful unique map of your country.

Washington	Oregon	Idaho
Population: 7,062,000 State Tree: Western Hemlock State Bird: Willow Goldfinch Marine Mammal: **Orca** State Fruit: Apple	Population: 4,000,000 State Tree: Douglas Fir State Bird: Western Meadowlark State Mammal: **American Beaver** State Nut: Hazelnut	Population: 1,650,000 State Tree: White Pine State Bird: Mountain Bluebird State Insect: **Monarch Butterfly** State Fruit: Huckleberry

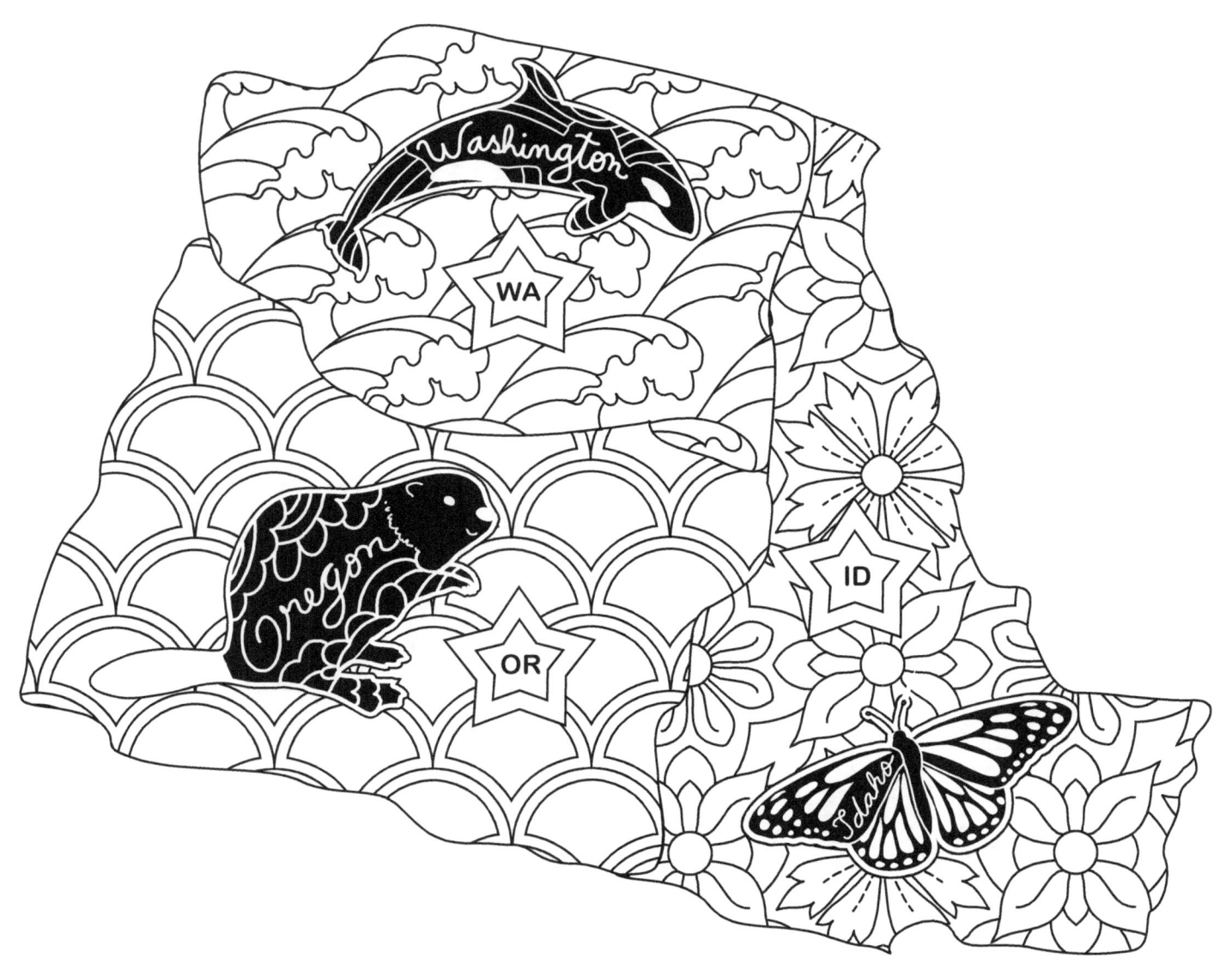

Montana	Wyoming
Population: 1,025,000	Population: 590,000
State Tree: Ponderosa Pine State Bird: Western Meadowlark State Mammal: ***Grizzly Bear***	State Tree: Plains Cottonwood State Bird: Western Meadowlark State Mammal: ***Bison*** State Fish: The Cutthroat Trout

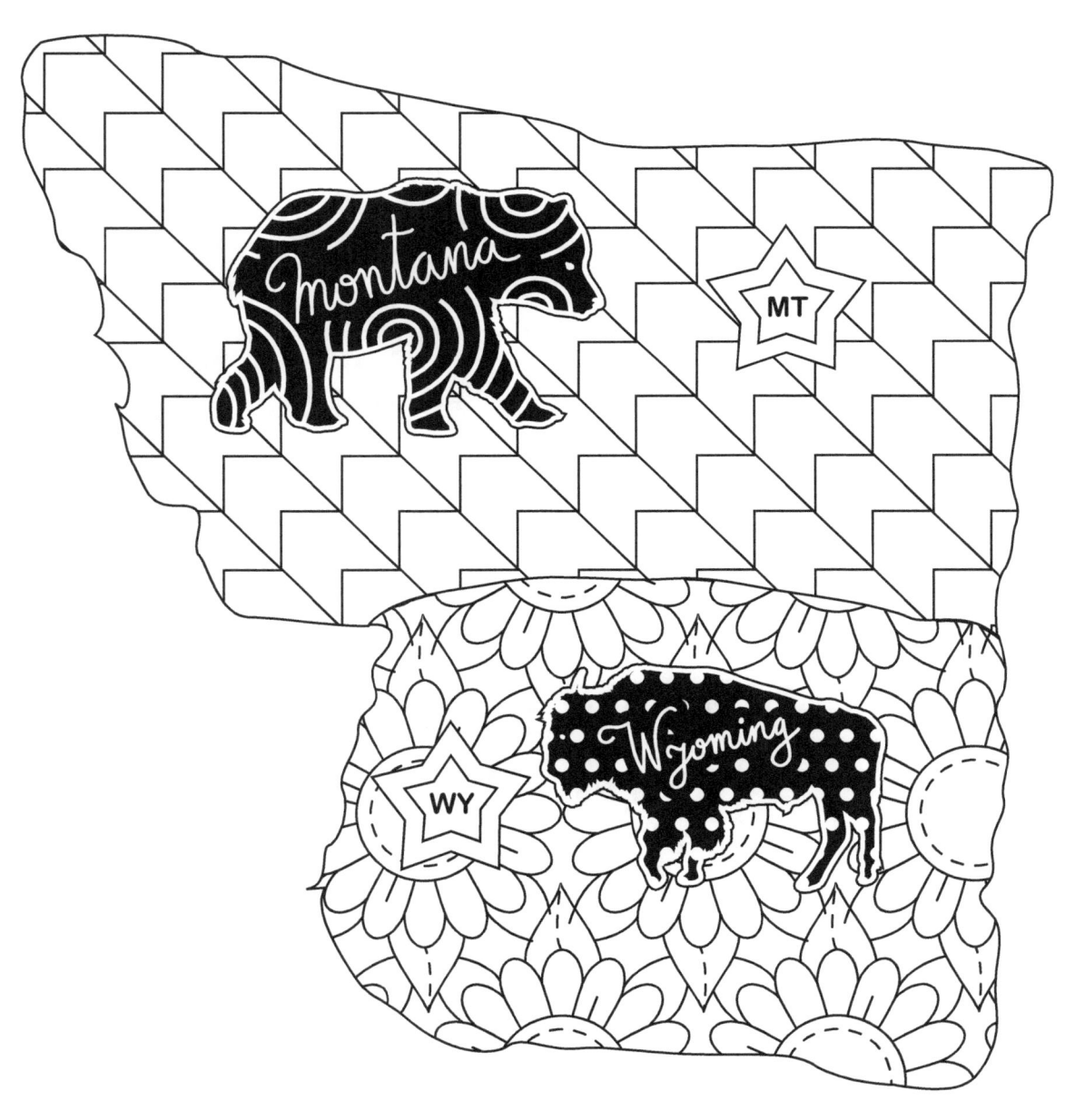

North Dakota	South Dakota	Nebraska
Population: 740,000 State Tree: American Elm State Bird: ***Western Meadowlark*** State Horse: Nakota State Fruit: Chokeberry	Population: 855,000 State Tree: Black Hills Spruce State Bird: Ringneck Pheasant State Mammal: ***Coyote*** State Insect: Honey Bee State Sport: Rodeo	Population: 1,890,000 State Tree: Cottonwood State Mammal: ***White-tailed Deer***

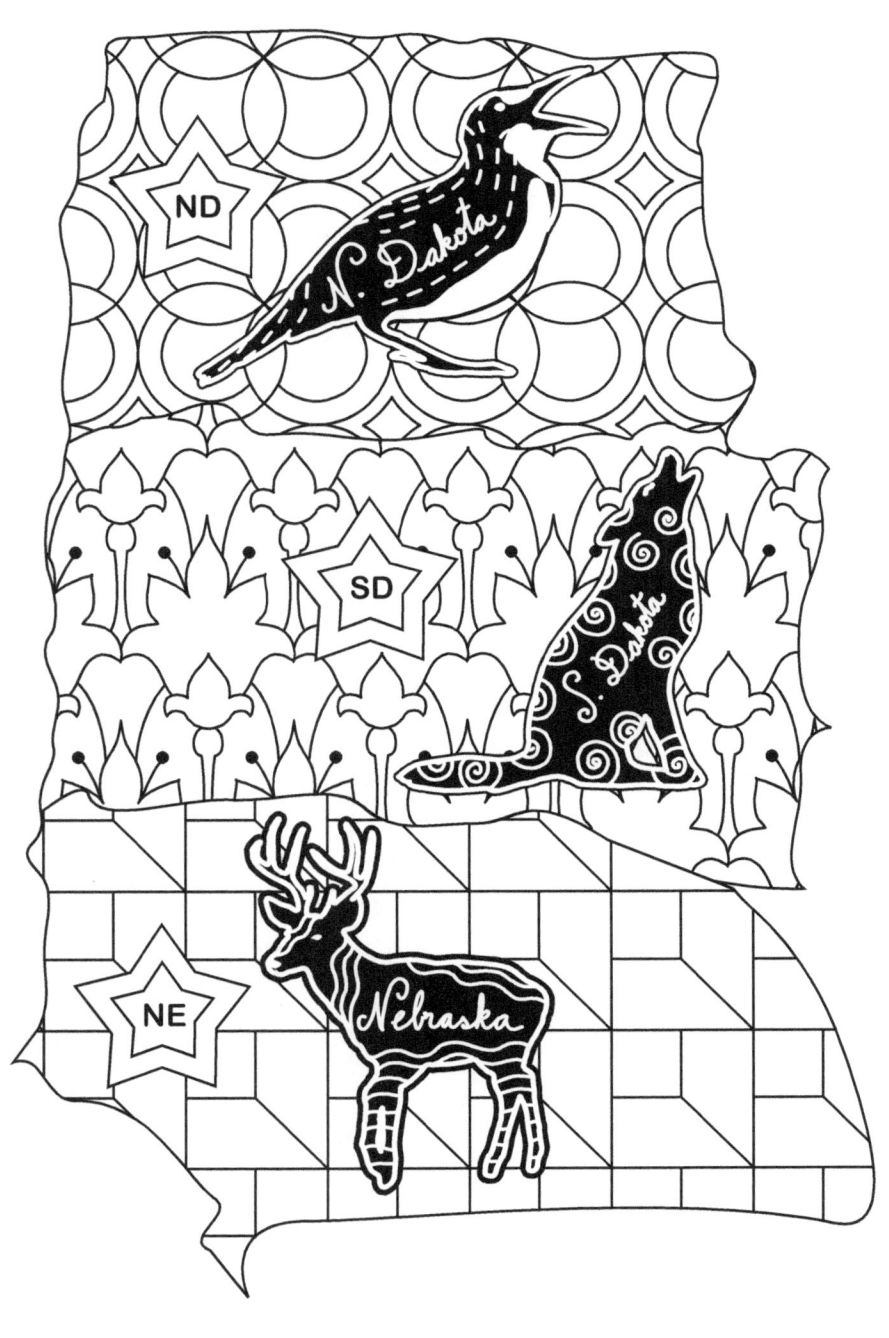

Minnesota	Iowa
Population: 5,460,000	Population: 3,110,000
State Tree: Red (Norway) Pine State Bird: Common Loon State Fruit: **Honeycrisp Apple**	State Tree: Oak State Bird: **Eastern Goldfinch** State Flower: Wild Prairie Rose

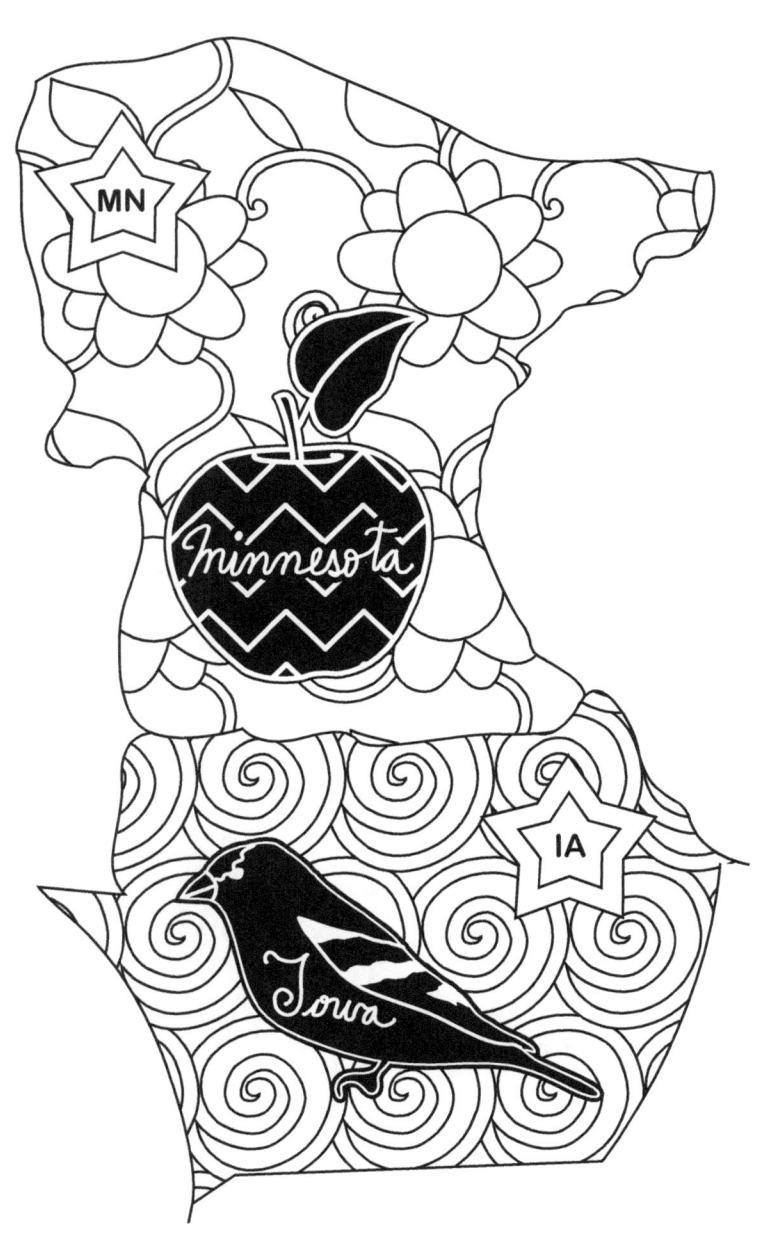

Wisconsin	Illinois
Population: 5,760,000 State Tree: Sugar Maple State Bird: Robin State Mammal: **Dairy Cow** State Insect: Honey Bee State Flower: Wood Violet	Population: 12,880,000 State Tree: Live Oak State Bird: Cardinal State Mammal: White-tailed Deer State Flower: **Violet**

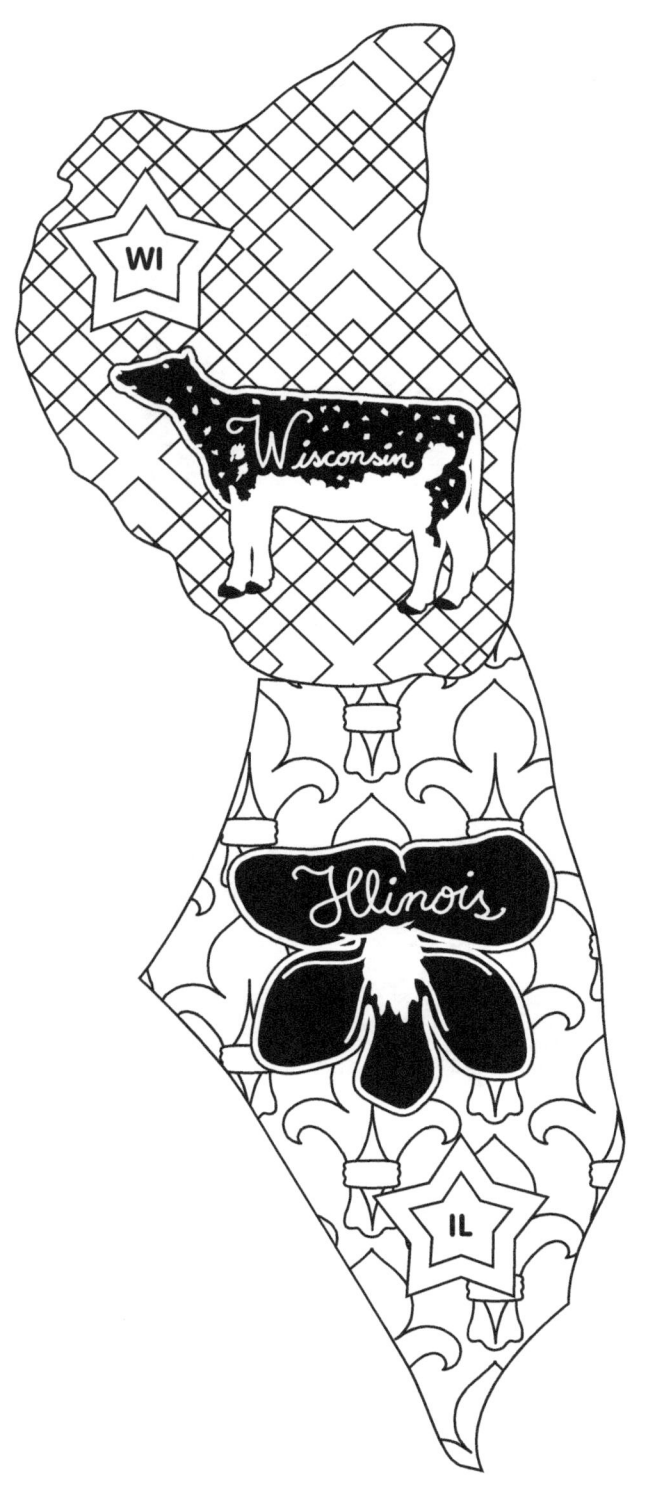

Michigan	Indiana
Population: 9,910,000	Population: 6,600,000
State Tree: Eastern White Pine State Bird: **Robin** State Mammal: White-tailed Deer State Flower: Apple Blossom	State Flower: **Peony**

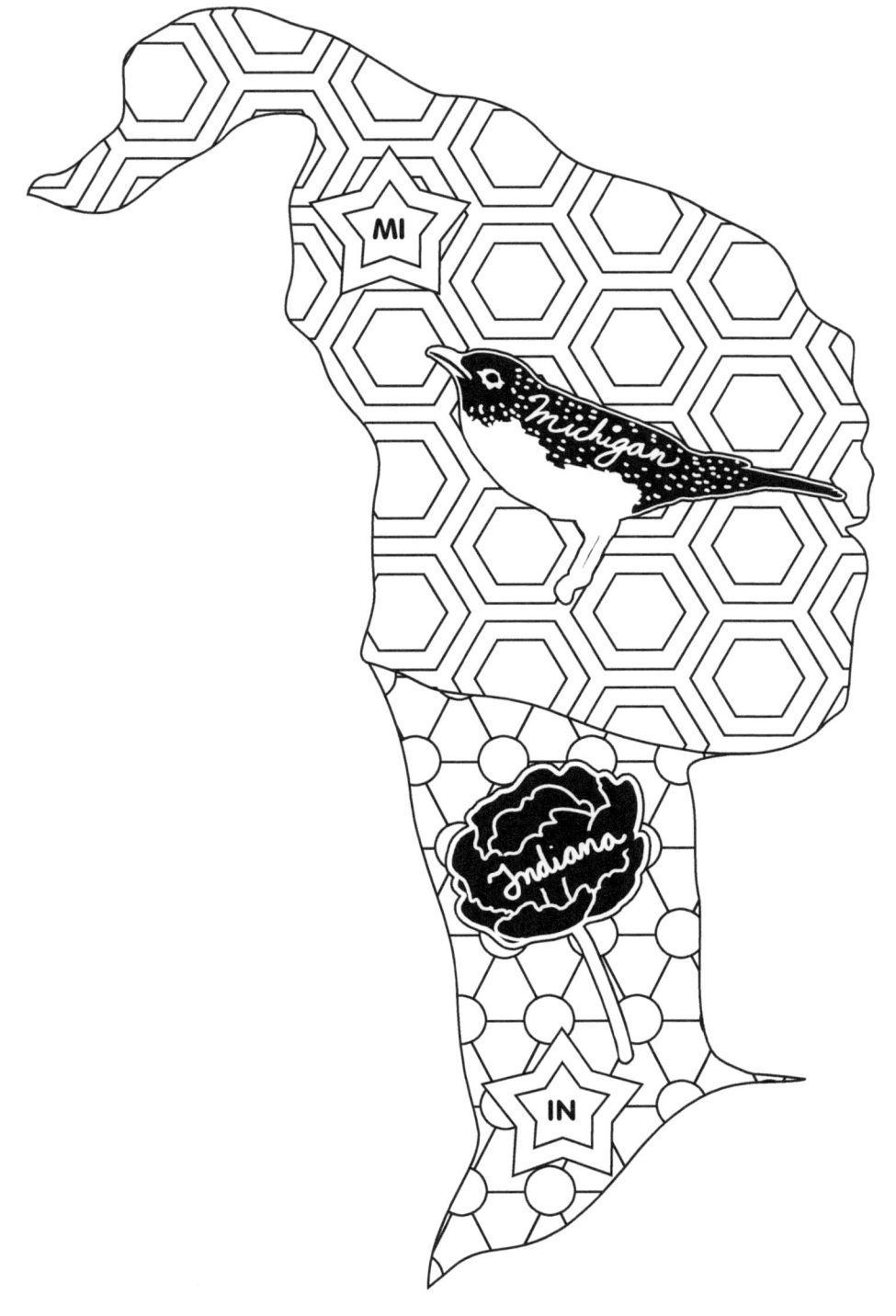

Maine	New Hampshire	Massachusetts
Population: 1,330,000	Population: 1,330,000	Population: 6,746,000
State Tree: White Pine State Bird: Chickadee State Mammal: *Moose* State Fruit: Apple	State Tree: White Birch State Bird: Purple Finch State Mammal: White-tailed Deer State Flower: *Purple Lilac*	State Tree: American Elm State Bird: *Chickadee* State Flower: Mayflower
New York	**Rhode Island**	**Connecticut**
Population: 19,750,000	Population: 1,055,000	Population: 3,597,000
State Tree: Sugar Maple State Bird: Bluebird State Mammal: Beaver State Fruit: *Apple* State Flower: Rose	State Tree: Red Maple State Bird: Rhode Island Red Hen State Flower: Violet	State Tree: White (Charter) Oak State Bird: American Robin State Marine Mammal: *Sperm Whale* State Insect: Praying Mantis
Vermont		
Population: 627,000		
State Tree: Sugar Maple State Bird: Hermit Thrush State Horse: *Morgan Horse* State Fruit: Apple State Flower: Red Clover		

California	Nevada
Population: 38,805,000	Population: 2,840,000
State Tree: **California Redwood** State Bird: California Valley Quail State Mammal: Grizzly Bear State Fish: Golden Trout	State Tree: Bristlecone Pine tate Bird: Mountain Bluebird State Mammal: **Desert Bighorn Sheep** State Flower: Sagebrush

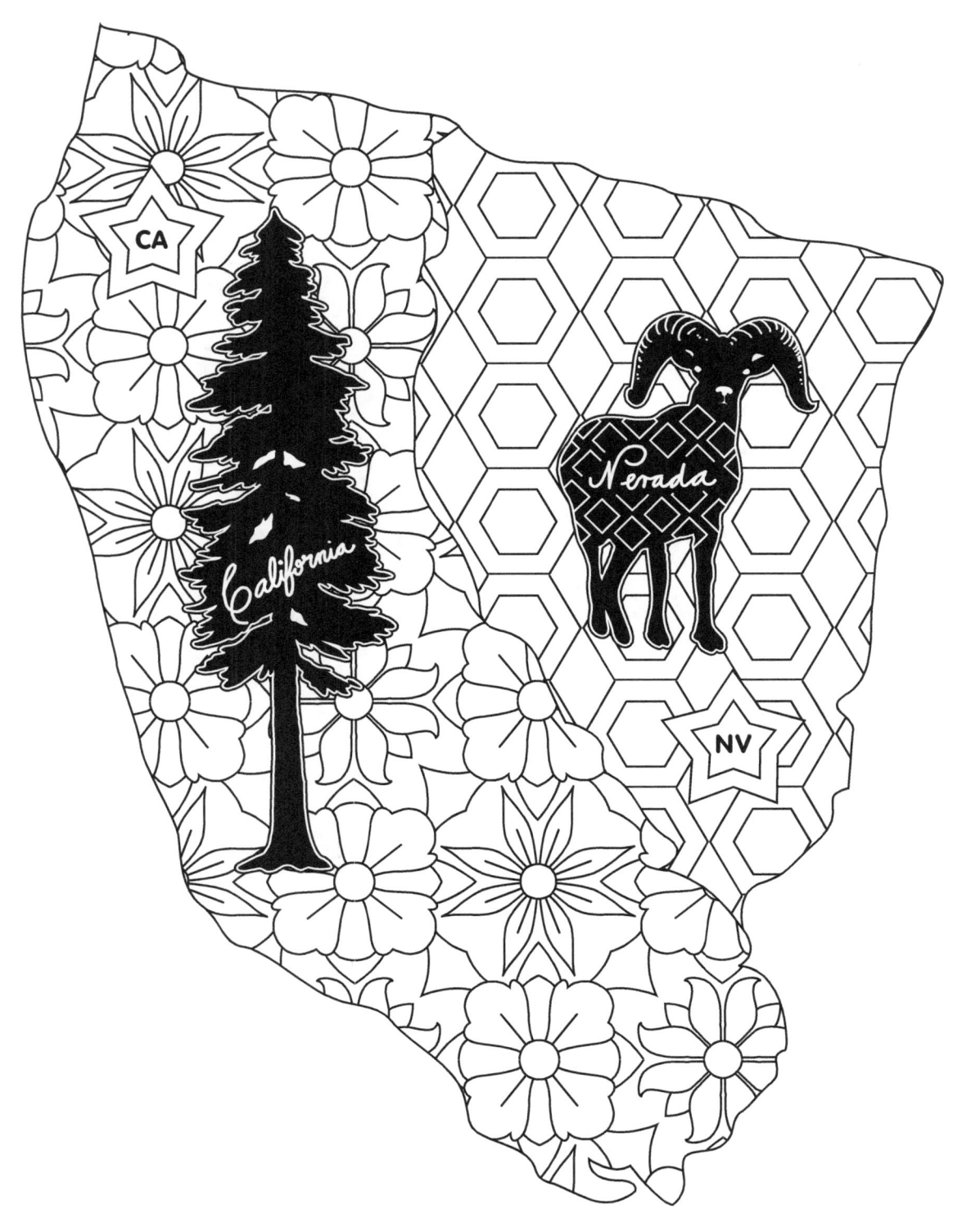

Utah	Arizona
Population: 2,945,000	Population: 6,735,000
State Tree: Blue Spruce State Bird: California Gull State Mammal: ***Rocky Mountain Elk***	State Tree: Palo Verde State Bird: Cactus Wren State Mammal: ***Ringtail Cat*** State Fish: Arizona Trout

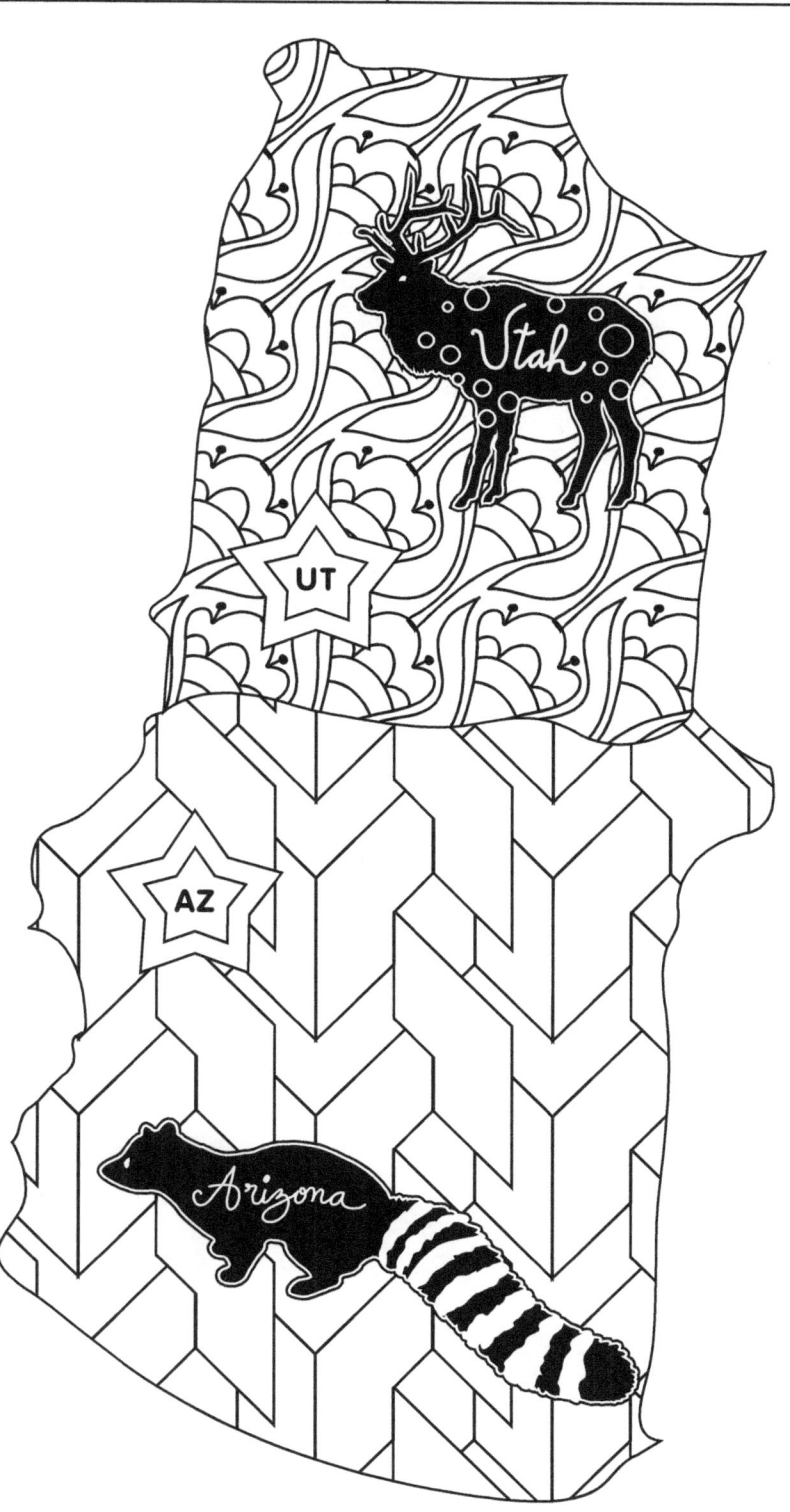

Colorado	New Mexico
Population: 5,360,000	Population: 2,086,000
State Tree: Colorado Blue Spruce State Bird: Lark Bunting State Mammal: Rocky Mountain Bighorn Sheep State Insect: **Colorado Hairstreak Butterfly** State Fish: Greenback Cutthroat Trout	State Tree: Piñon State Bird: **Roadrunner** State Mammal: Black Bear State Flower: Yucca

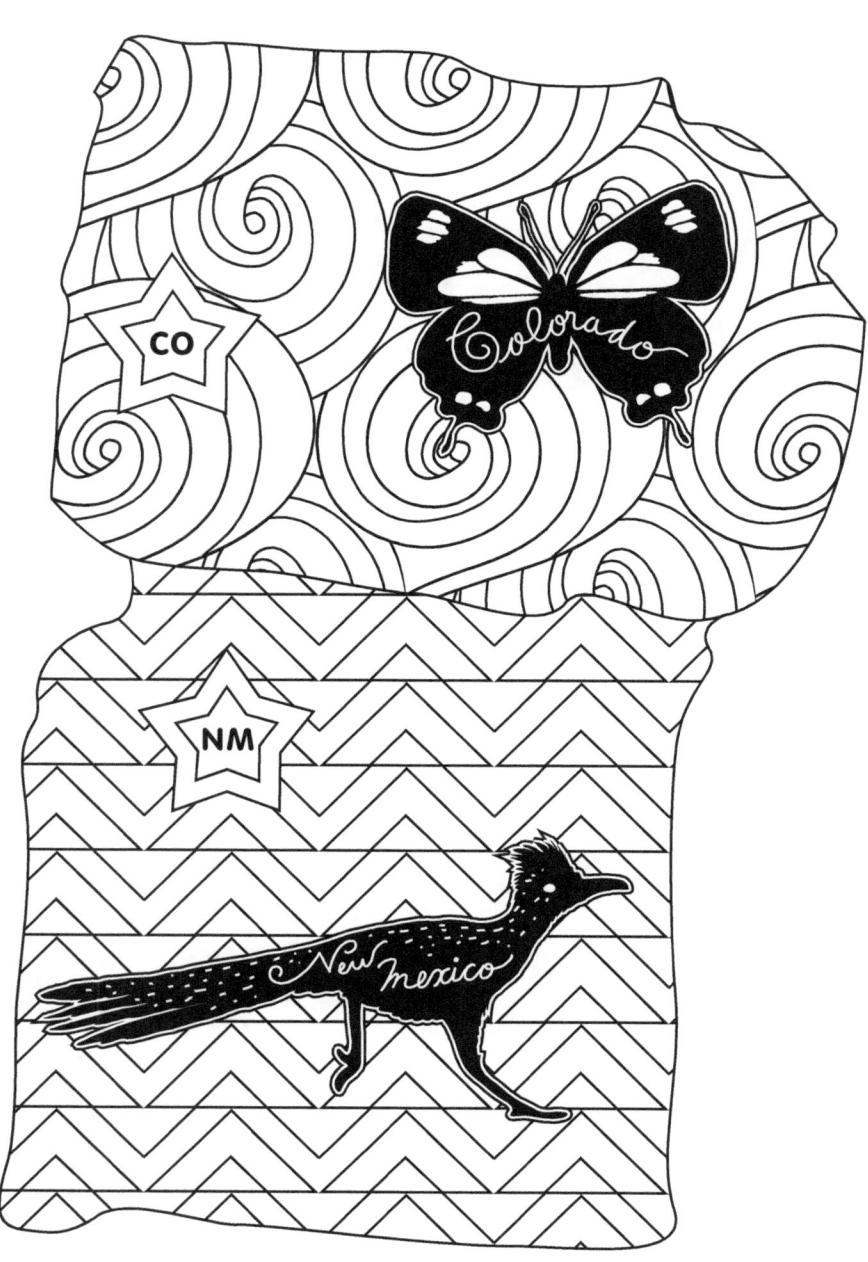

Kansas	Oklahoma
Population: 2,905,000	Population: 3,880,000
State Tree: Cottonwood State Bird: Western Meadowlark State Mammal: **Buffalo** State Flower: Sunflower	State Tree: Redbud State Bird: ***Scissor-Tailed Flycatcher*** State Mammal: Bison State Flower: Mistletoe

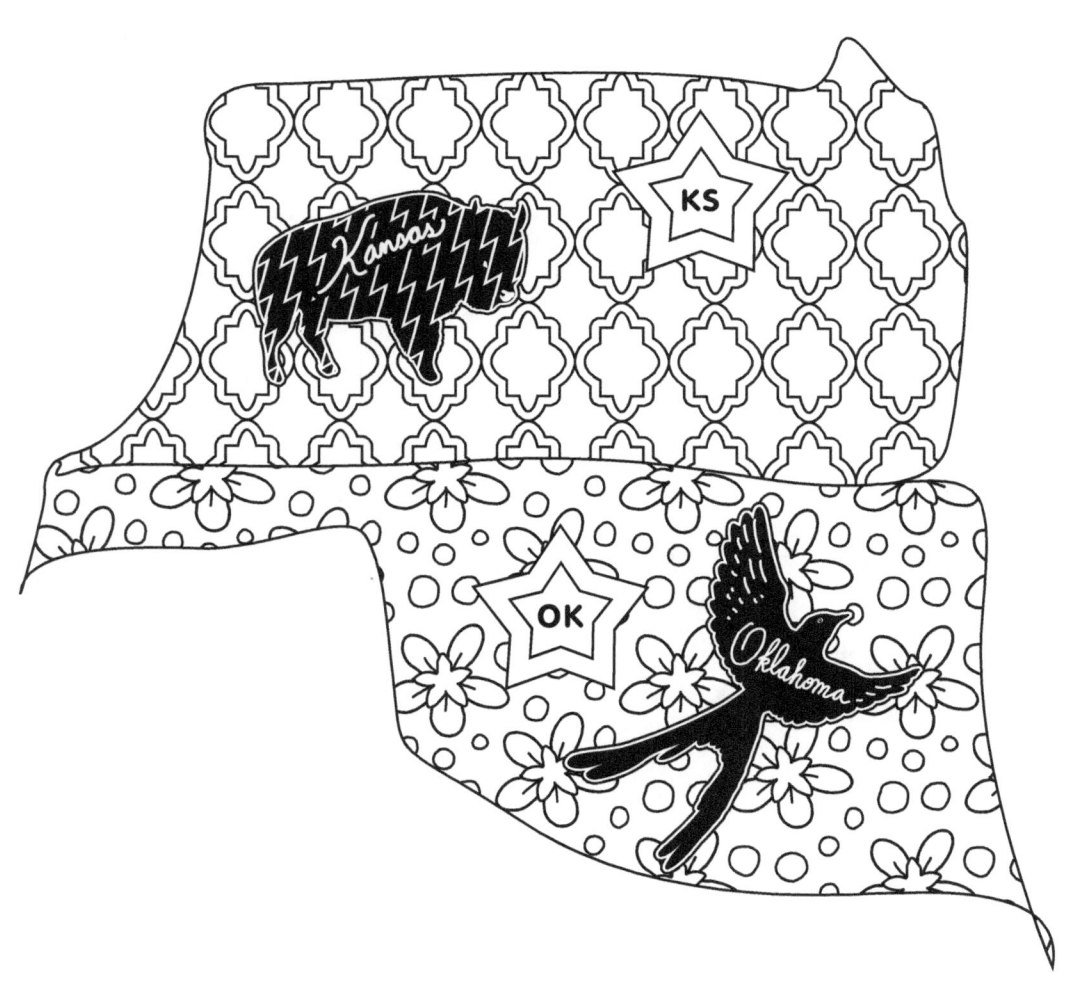

Missouri	Arkansas
Population: 6,065,000	Population: 2,970,000
State Tree: Dogwood	State Tree: Loblolly Pine
State Bird: Bluebird	State Bird: Mockingbird
State Mammal: **Mule**	State Mammal: White-tailed Deer
State Horse: Missouri Fox Trotter	State Insect: Honeybee
State Flower: Hawthorn	State Instrument: **Fiddle**

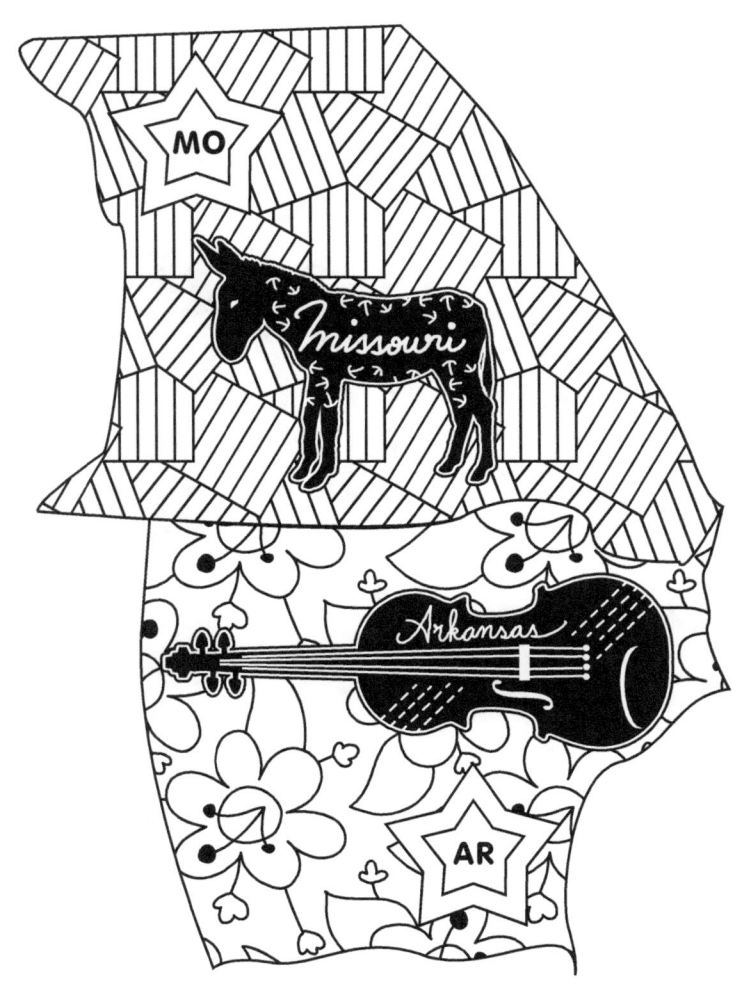

Texas

Population: 26,960,000

State Tree: Pecan
State Bird: Mockingbird
State Mammal: *Texas Longhorn*
State Flower: Bluebonnet

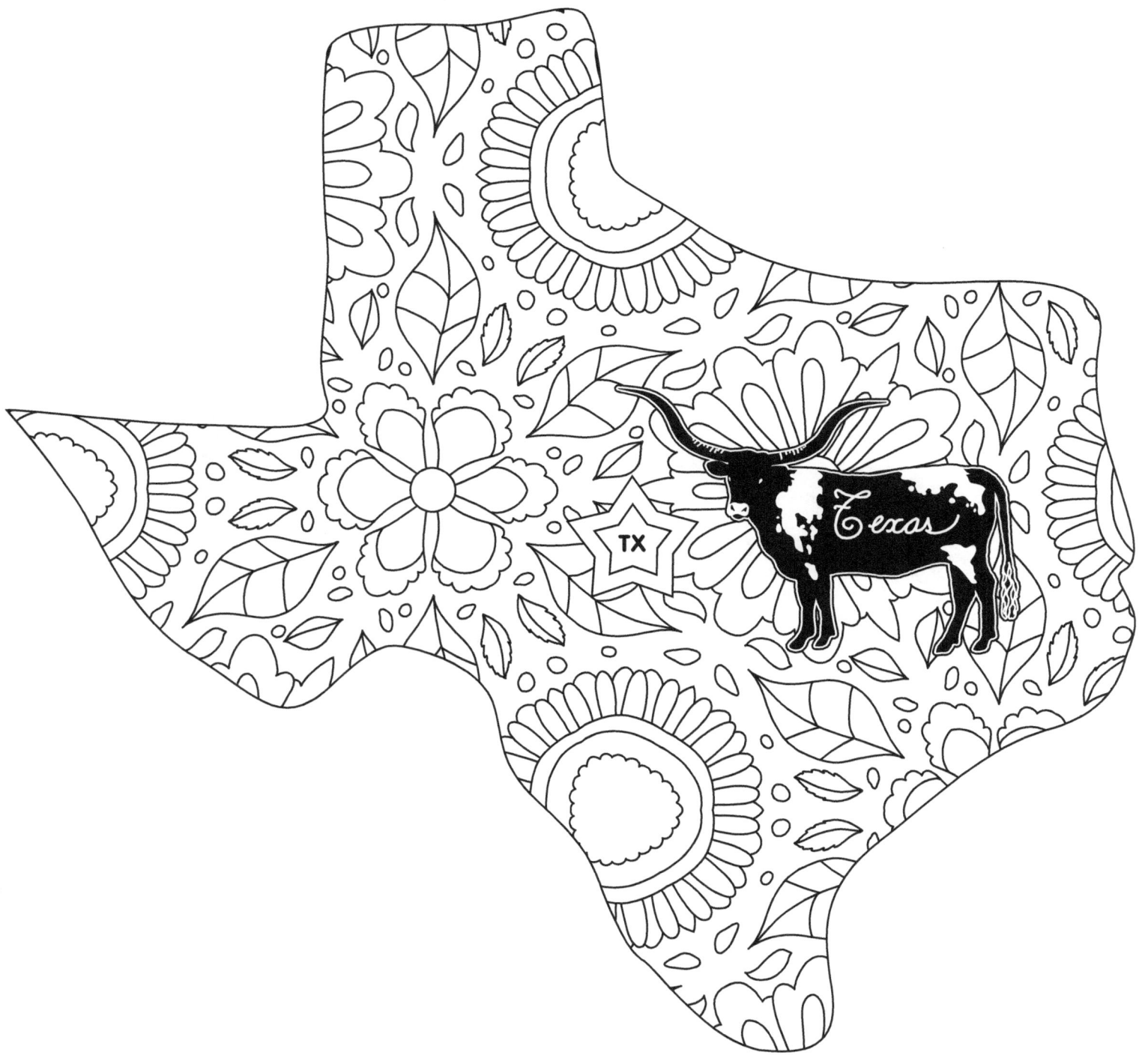

Lousiana	Mississippi	Alabama
Population: 4,650,000 State Tree: Bald Cypress State Bird: **Eastern Brown Pelican** State Mammal: Louisiana Black Bear	Population: 2,995,000 State Tree: Magnolia State Bird: Mockingbird State Waterfowl: ***Wood Duck*** State Nut: Hazelnut State Flower: Magnolia	Population: 4,850,000 State Tree: Southern Longleaf Pine State Bird: Wild Turkey State Mammal: ***Alabama Red-bellied Turtle***

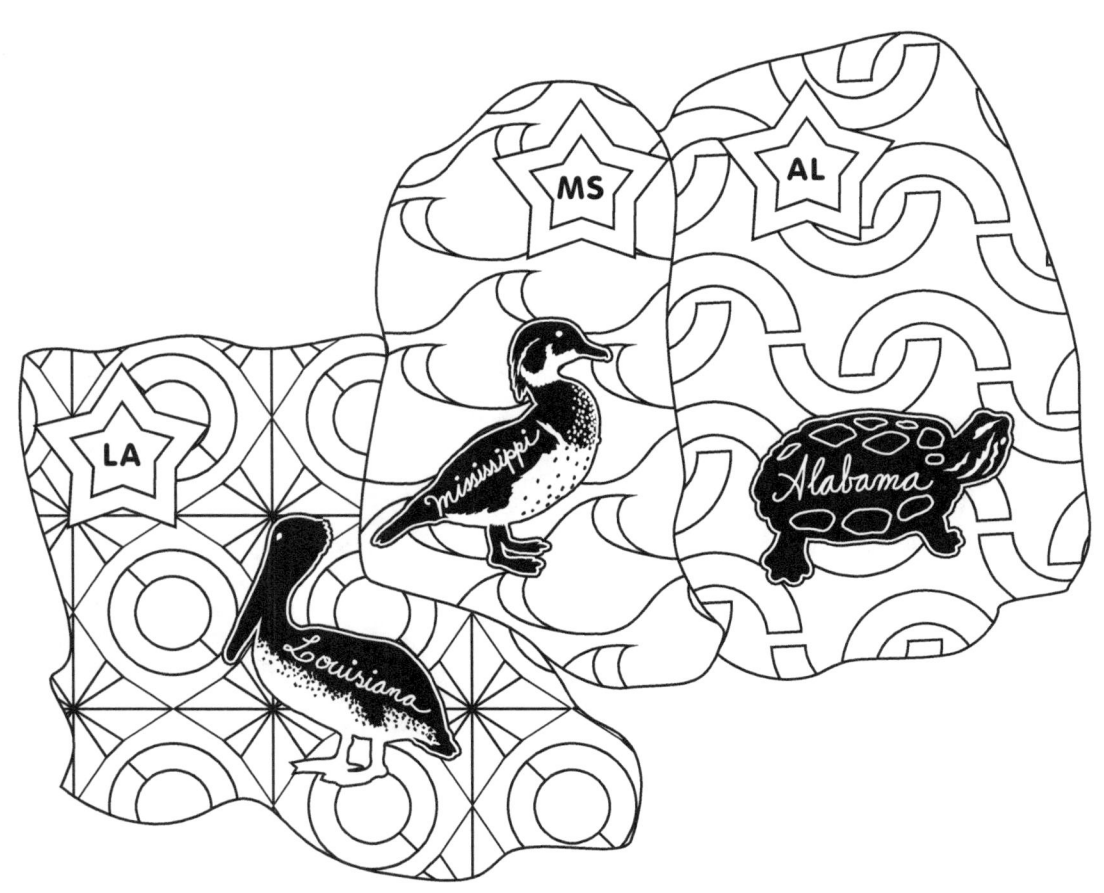

Ohio	Kentucky	Tennessee
Population: 11,600,000 State Tree: Buckeye State Bird: Cardinal State Flower: **Scarlet Carnation**	Population: 4,450,000 State Tree: Tulip Poplar State Bird: Cardinal State Mammal: **Gray Squirrel** State Flower: Goldenrod	Population: 6,550,000 State Tree: Tulip Poplar State Bird: Mockingbird State Mammal: **Raccoon** State Flower: Iris

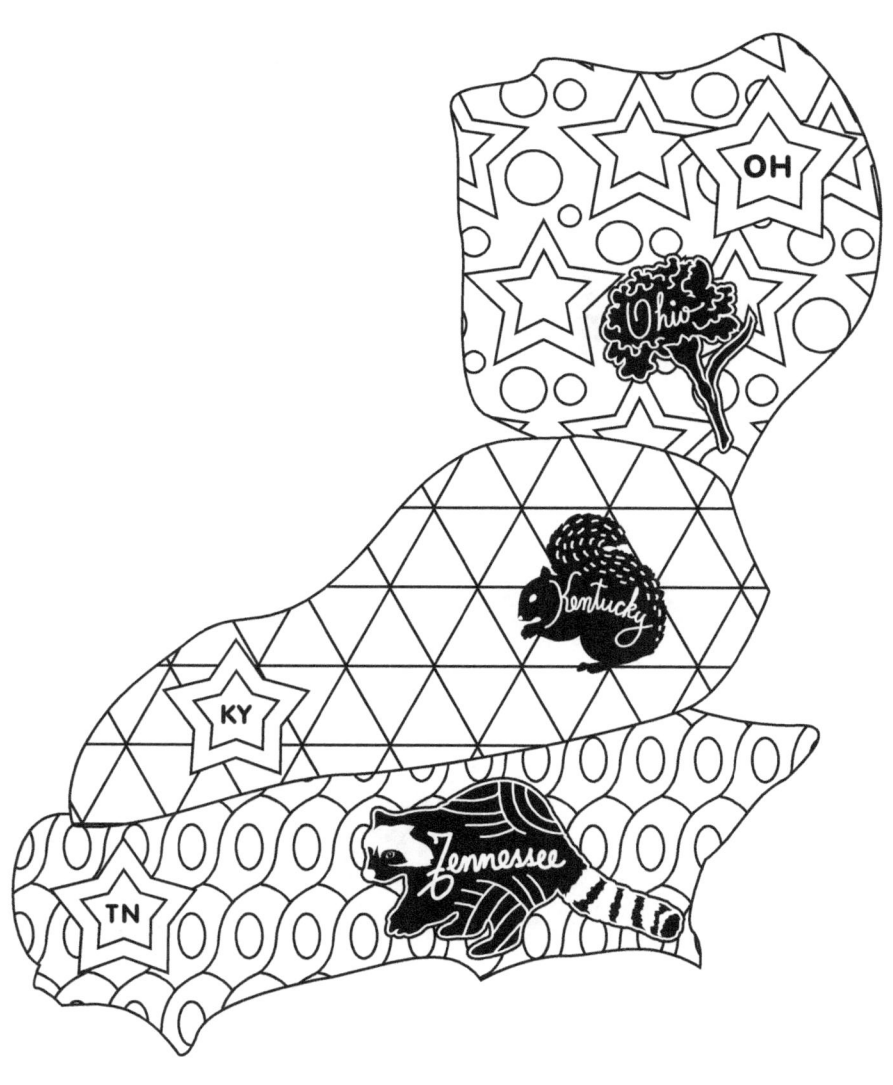

Georgia	Florida
Population: 10,098,000 State Tree: Southern Live Oak State Bird: Brown Thrasher State Mammal: Right Whale State Fruit: **Peach** State Flower: Cherokee Rose	Population: 19,895,000 State Tree: Sabal Palmetto Palm State Bird: Mockingbird State Mammal: **Panther (Puma)** State Flower: Orange Blossom

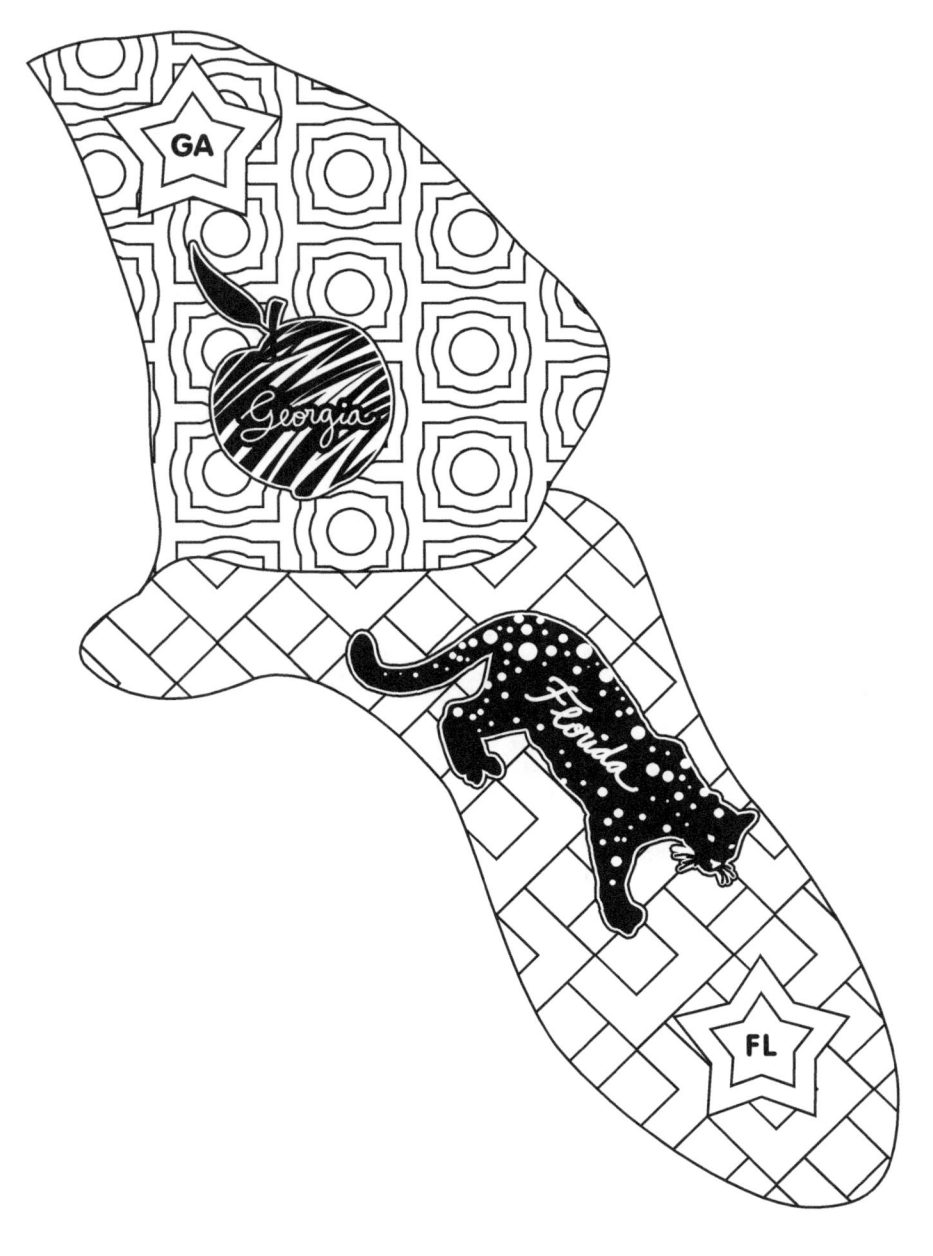

West Virginia	Pennsylvania	New Jersey
Population: 1,850,000	Population: 12,790,000	Population: 8,940,000
State Tree: Sugar Maple State Bird: Cardinal Marine Mammal: Black Bear State Fish: **Brook Trout** State Fruit: Golden Delicious	State Tree: Hemlock State Bird: Ruffed Grouse State Dog: **Great Dane** State Flower: Mountain Laurel	State Tree: **Red Oak** State Bird: Eastern Goldfinch State Mammal: Horse State Flower: Purple Violet

Delaware	Maryland
Population: 936,000	Population: 5,980,000
State Tree: American Holly State Bird: **Blue Hen Chicken** State Fish: Weakfish State Flower: Peach Blossom	State Tree: White Oak State Bird: Baltimore Oriole State Mammel: **Cat Calico** State Flower: Black-Eyed Susan

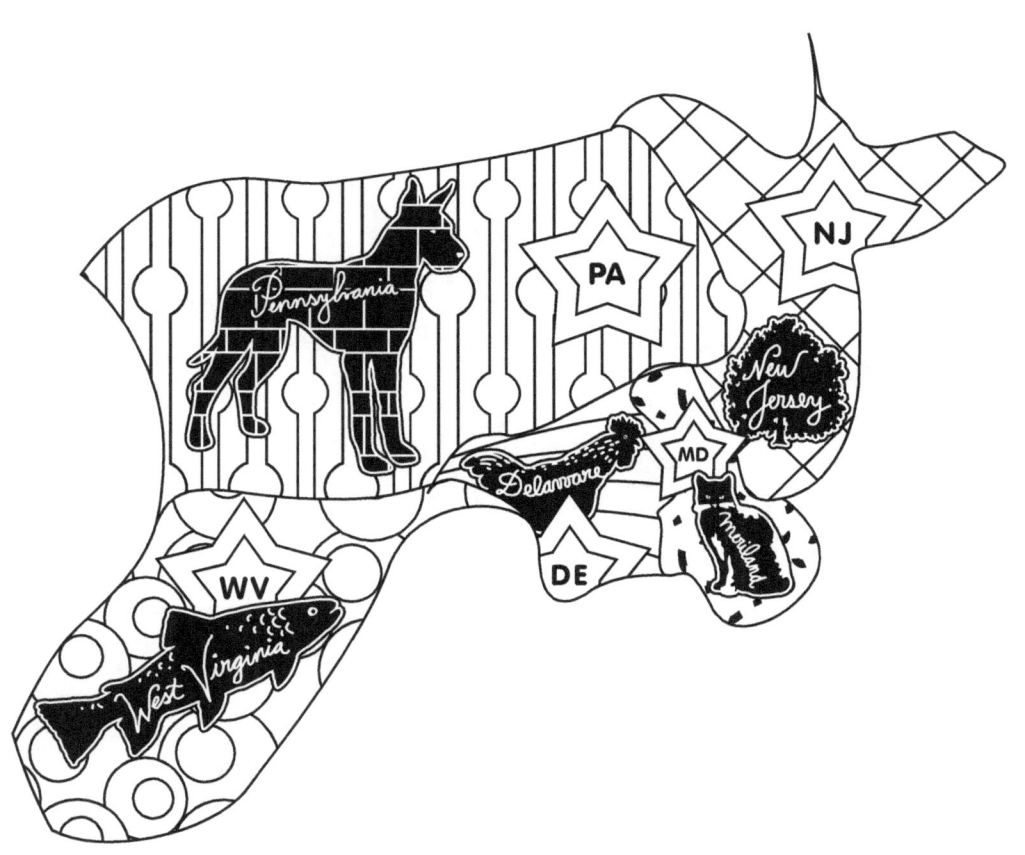

Virginia	North Carolina	South Carolina
Population: 8,330,000 State Tree: Dogwood State Bird: Cardinal Marine Mammal: Foxhound State Insect: *Tiger Swallowtail Butterfly*	Population: 9,945,000 State Tree: Longleaf Pine State Bird: Cardinal State Mammal: Gray Squirrel State Flower: *Dogwood*	Population: 4,835,000 State Tree: Cabbage Palmetto State Bird: *Carolina Wren* State Mammal: White-tailed Deer State Fflower: Yellow Jessamine

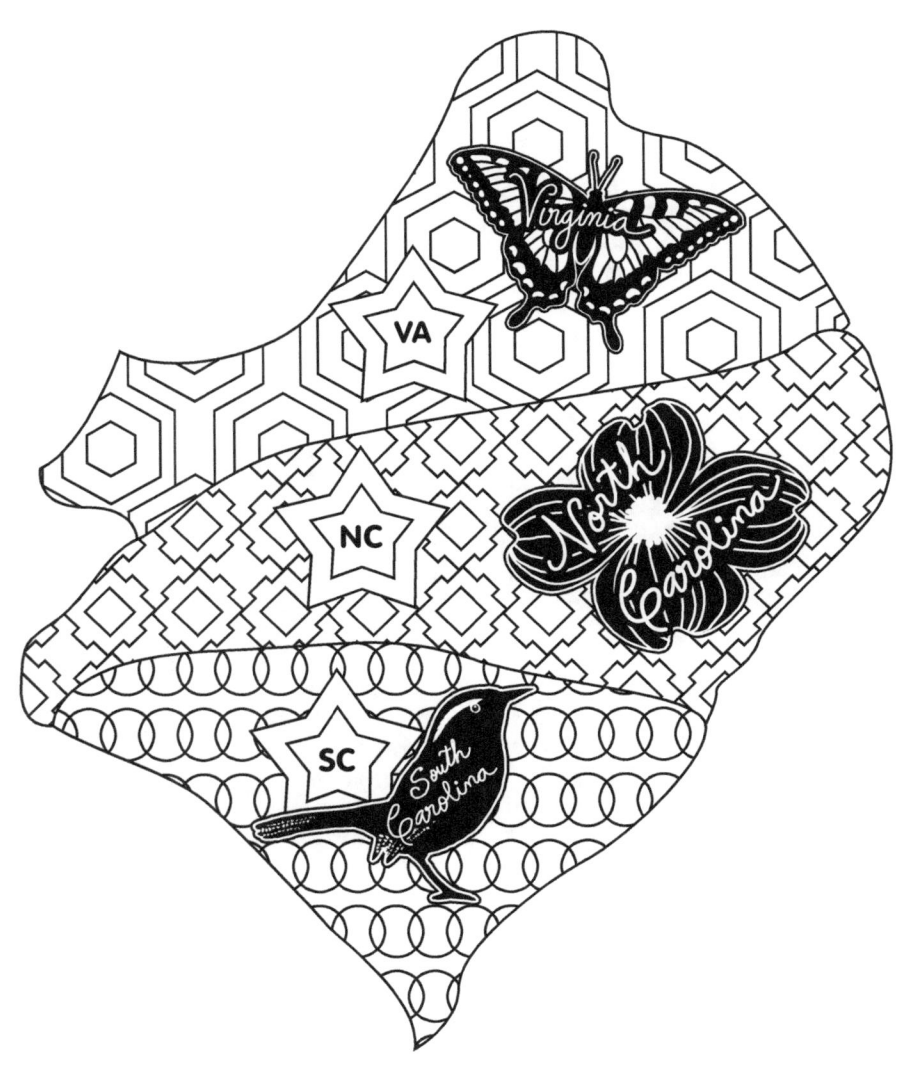

Alaska

Population: 750,000

State Tree: Sitka Spruce
State Bird: Willow Ptarmigan
State Marine Mammel: **_Bowhead Whale_**
State Flower: Forget-me-not

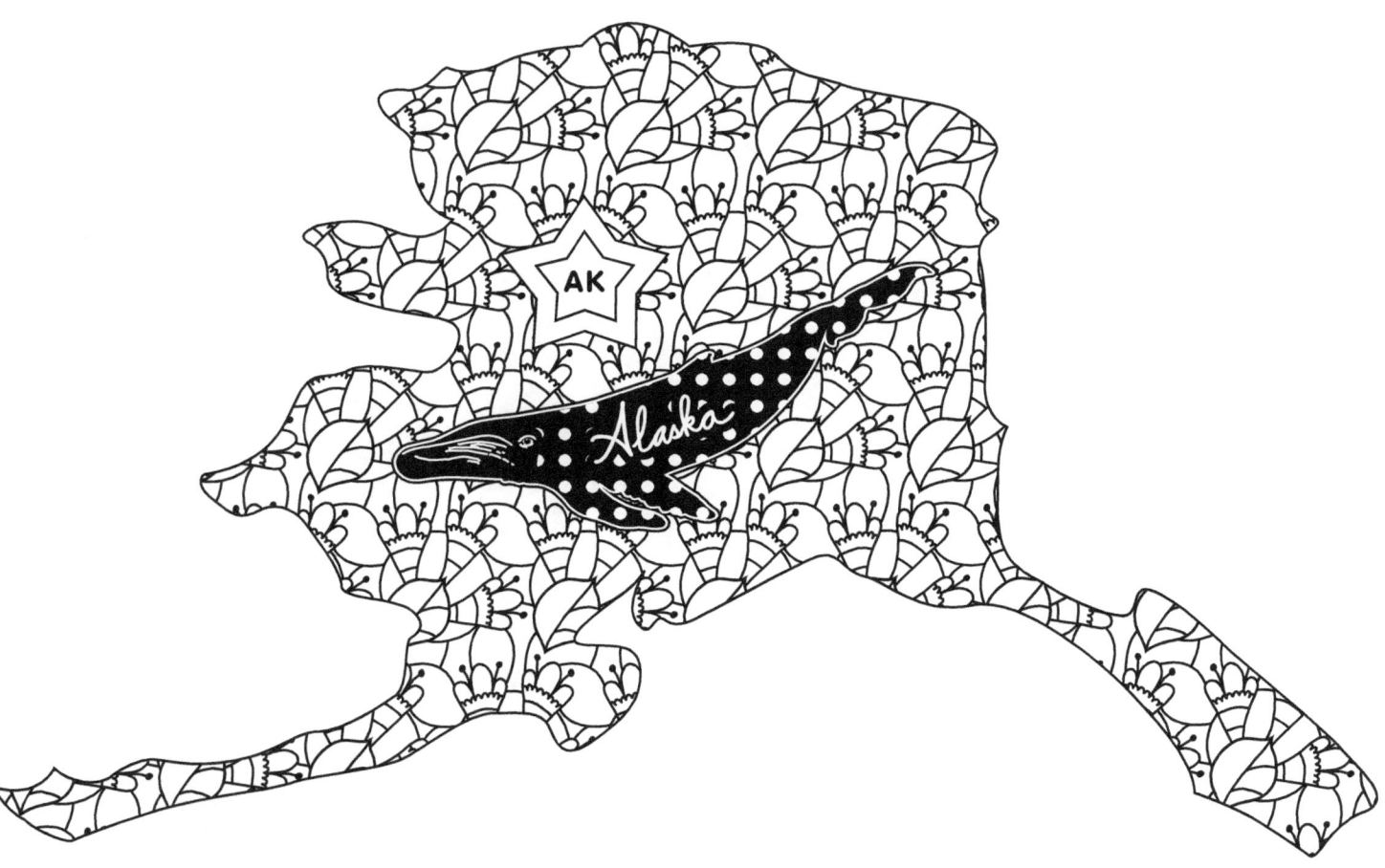

Hawaii

Population: 1,420,000

State Tree: Kukui (Candlenut)
State Bird: **Nene (Hawaiian Goose)**
State Marine Mammel: Humpback Whale
State Flower: Yellow Hibiscus

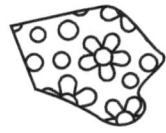
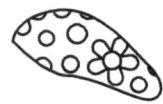
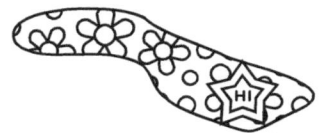
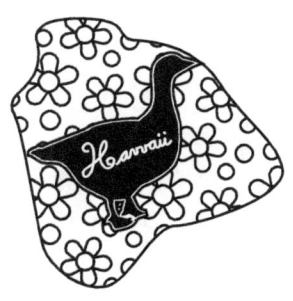